VEGETARIAN

VEGETARIAN RECIPES FOR
THE ADVENTUROUS COOK

VEGETARIAN

VEGETARIAN RECIPES FOR
THE ADVENTUROUS COOK

Quantum
Books

A QUANTUM BOOK

Published by
Quantum Books Ltd
6 Blundell Street
London N7 9BH

1-86160-190-5

Project Manager: Rebecca Kingsley
Designer: Bruce Low
Editor: Sarah Harris

The material in this publication previously appeared in
*Healthy Vegetarian Cooking and Vegetarian
Pasta Cookbook*

QUMVEG
Set in Fritz Quadrata
Reproduced in Singapore by Eray Scan
Printed in Singapore by Star Standard Industries (Pte) Ltd

Contents

····

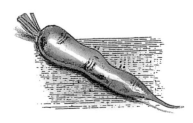

INTRODUCTION

Vegetarian cookery, once viewed with mistrust as appropriate only for those pursuing an alternative, often radical, lifestyle, whether religious or secular, is now respected and accepted throughout the world.

The ready availability of fresh fruits and vegetables, together with an almost bewildering array of prepared meals, means that following a vegetarian diet, whether wholly or partially is extremely easy. Even restaurants, whose only concession to vegetarians was perhaps a salad or bland pasta only a few years ago, are now offering a wide variety of interesting and delicious vegetable dish-es for those who choose not to eat meat.

For many years, traditional food has been stodgy and high in fat, and the continual emergence of more and more highly processed junk foods meant that natural, wholefoods were almost the exception, rather than the norm. Yet in today's health-conscious environment, we are now actively encouraged to move away from high-fat, high-cholesterol meals. Vegetarian food, rich in vitamins, minerals and fibre and generally lower in calories, is an ideal alternative. A balanced vegetarian diet can provide all the nutrients we need for a healthy, active life.

The sheer variety of ingredients that are available today make it possible to prepare a diverse range of tasty and healthy recipes without meat. No longer is vegetarian food looked down upon as bland and boring. Instead we can liven up our mealtimes with dishes that incorporate spices and seasonings from around the world, which have the added benefit of meeting all our nutritional requirements.

The general acceptance and embracing of vegetarian food today has been influenced by several factors, some

modern, some rooted in history. The desire for a healthier eating plan has certainly played a part in changing attitudes, as have the meat-related health scares in recent years and revelations about the sometimes inhumane methods of rearing and slaughtering animals for food.

Many religions, particularly the Hindu and Buddhist faiths, have advocated vegetarianism for centuries, as one of their central philosophies is that all animal life is sacred. In today's society many people are turning to spirituality, and embracing such beliefs as they do so.

Yet such convictions are frequently found among people whose beliefs are not based on religious thought or practice. Many people, particularly teenagers, have at one time or the other decided to exclude meat from their meals, and many continue to do so, believing that killing animals for food is morally unacceptable.

In reality, the use of the term vegetarian can sometimes be confusing, as people often tend to believe they are vegetarian simply if they have cut red meat from their diet. In fact, vegetarianism excludes all meat - red and white, including fish and poultry. Lacto-vegetarians will also not eat eggs, although dairy products such as cheese and milk are allowed. Vegans take

a step further, and exclude all animal-based foods from their diet. This includes all dairy produce and anything containing gelatine.

Whether for health, moral or religious reasons, the number of people who are choosing to cut down on meat-based foods, and turning to vegetable and pulse dishes - a diet that could be accurately described as demi-vegetarian - is large, and still growing.

MAINTAINING A HEALTHY DIET

Simply cutting out meat and substituting vegetables and salads alone will not make for a healthy diet. Pulses and cereals should also be incorporated to help provide the correct balance of vitamins, minerals, proteins and fibre.

One of the most important ingredients in a vegetarian diet is fibre - essential for the effective working of the digestive system which processes our food. In today's society of over-processed junk-food, fibre is often an ingredient that is sorely lacking.

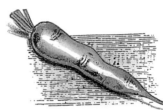

The lack of protein that has often caused health problems in vegetarians in the past is now easily remedied, with the increase in availability of vegetable protein foods such as soya or tofu. Incorporated into Oriental cooking for thousands of years, these products are gaining wider acceptance in the Western world - as the proliferation and popularity of Chinese and Japanese restaurants would suggest!

Fats, although an essential part of our diet in moderation, are often used to excess in modern cookery. While cutting out meat will reduce fat intake, many of the vegetarian substitutes - such as nuts - are also high in fat. Grilling or stir frying, rather than deep frying can often help.

Fats can be divided into three categories. Saturated fats have the worst publicity, linked as they are to cholesterol-related illnesses. These are hard fats and generally derived from meat products. Polyunsaturated fats - oils and soft spreads - are generally vegetable-based. Mono-unsaturated fats are generally agreed to be the healthiest option, as they have a beneficial effect on cholesterol levels. These include olive oil and avocados. However, despite their benefits, the key word - as with all fats - should still be - moderation.

One of the complaints sometimes aimed at vegetarian food is that it is bland and tasteless. Yet this need not be the case, as the inventive use of herbs and spices can transform even the most rudimentary vegetable dish. Fresh herbs naturally have the best flavour, but unless you have your own herb garden, they are often difficult to find and expensive.

The art of vegetarian cookery lies in the subtle and innovative combination of textures and flavours to make delicious and nutritionally well-balanced meals. The recipes selected for this cookbook use a variety of ingredients to create tasty and versatile dishes that will tempt vegetarians and non-vegetarians alike.

For ease of reference, the recipes have been divided into four categories: soups and starters; pasta; side dishes and desserts.

CHAPTER ONE

SOUPS AND STARTERS

BORSCHT

■

CREAMY GARLIC MUSHROOMS

■

AVOCADO AND
POMEGRANATE SALAD

■

ONION, LENTIL AND LEMON SOUP

BORSCHT

SERVES 6

INGREDIENTS

2 large onions

3 large beets

3 large carrots

2 parsnips

4 stalks celery

3 tbsp tomato paste

4 large tomatoes

½ small white cabbage, shredded

1 tbsp honey

1 tbsp lemon juice

salt and freshly ground black pepper

handful of chopped parsley

plain white flour

low-fat sour cream or yogurt

Quintessentially Russian, borscht is a fresh-tasting, healthy soup which can be served hot or cold depending on the occasion. Beet is a naturally sweet vegetable, and gives the soup a unique flavour.

Cut onions, beet, carrots, parsnips, and celery into matchsticks. Bring a large pan of salted water to a boil, add the tomato paste and the vegetables and simmer for 30 minutes until tender.

Skin the tomatoes, remove the seeds, and chop. Add to the pan with the cabbage, honey, lemon juice, and seasoning. Simmer for 5 minutes, then throw in a handful of chopped parsley. Check seasoning.

If necessary, thicken the soup with a blend of a little flour and low-fat sour cream. The soup is best made the day before it is to be eaten. Reheat and serve with a bowl of low-fat sour cream or yogurt.

CREAMY GARLIC MUSHROOMS

SERVES 4

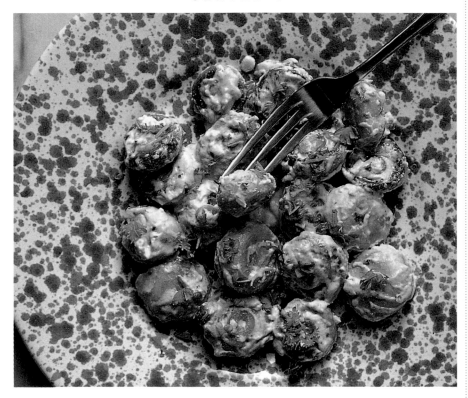

INGREDIENTS

2 tbsp olive oil

1 large garlic clove, crushed

2 spring onions, chopped

salt and freshly ground black pepper

12 oz button mushrooms

6 oz low-fat soft cheese

a little parsley, chopped (optional)

These are perfect baked-potato fillers!

Heat the oil in a large frying pan. Add the garlic, spring onions, and seasoning, and cook for 2 minutes. Then add all the mushrooms and toss them over high heat for a couple of minutes, until they are hot. Do not cook the mushrooms until their juices run as they will be too watery.

AVOCADO AND POMEGRANATE SALAD

SERVES 4

INGREDIENTS

1 ripe pomegranate, cut in half
50g (2oz) black grapes, cut in half
and seeded
2 small ripe avocados
1 tbsp lemon juice

Dressing

4 tbsp white-wine vinegar
2 tbsp orange juice
salt and freshly ground black pepper
1 tsp honey
1 tsp olive oil
1 tbsp peanut or sunflower oil
2 tbsp chopped fresh mint

Garnish

fresh mint leaves

In a small bowl, whisk together wine vinegar, orange juice, salt and pepper to taste and honey. Slowly whisk in olive oil and vegetable oil until dressing is thick and creamy. Stir in the chopped mint. Set aside.

Into a medium bowl, scrape seeds out of pomegranate halves. Add grape halves and toss to mix.

Cut avocados in half and remove pits. Using a round-bladed knife, run it between skin and flesh of avocados, working skin away from flesh until skin is removed.

Place avocados, round-side up, on work surface and, using a sharp knife and starting ½ inch below stem end, cut avocado lengthwise into ¼-inch slices, leaving stem end intact. Arrange each sliced avocado half on 4 individual plates. Using palm of hand, gently push avocado slices forward to fan out slices. Sprinkle lemon juice over them.

Sprinkle a quarter of the pomegranate seed-grape mixture on to each avocado half and spoon over dressing. Garnish each plate with a few mint leaves.

ONION, LENTIL AND LEMON SOUP

SERVES 4

INGREDIENTS

300 ml (½ pt) water
25g (1oz cup) plus 1 tbsp pearl barley
1 tbsp tomato paste
1½l (2½ pt) vegetable stock
12g (½ oz) lentils, rinsed and picked over
5 onions, sliced very thinly
1 tsp dried anise seeds
juice of 1 large lemon
large pinch of sweet paprika
pinch of cayenne pepper
salt and freshly ground black pepper

Garnish

12 paper-thin lemon slices

Barley and lentils are two Armenian favourites paired in this earthy soup. Served with warm cornbread, it would make a filling supper or lunch.

Bring the water to a boil in a large enamelled or stainless steel saucepan. Stir in the barley, cover, and simmer over low heat for about 20–25 minutes, until the barley is just tender and the water has been absorbed. Stir in the tomato paste, vegetable stock, lentils, onions, and anise. Bring to the boil, cover, and simmer over low heat for 1 hour, or until the lentils are soft.

Stir in the lemon juice, paprika, cayenne pepper, and salt and pepper to taste, and simmer uncovered for a further 20 minutes. Pour the soup into heated bowls, and garnish each with two very thin slices of lemon.

CHAPTER TWO

PASTA

CREAMY LEEK AND PASTA FLAN

■

BABY CAULIFLOWER AND BROCCOLI CHEESE

■

PROVENÇAL GREEN BEANS WITH PASTA

■

PASTA PAELLA

■

SPINACH AND MUSHROOM LASAGNE

■

VERDI VEGETABLES WITH VERMICELLI

■

STUFFED COURGETTES

■

GNOCCHETTI SARDI WITH BROCCOLI
AND TOMATOES

■

TOMATO AND PASTA SALAD

■

ASPARAGUS RAVIOLI WITH TOMATO SAUCE

CREAMY LEEK AND PASTA FLAN

SERVES 6–8

INGREDIENTS

100 g (4 oz) dried orecchiette (ears)

dash of olive oil, plus 45 ml (3 tbsp)

a little flour, for dredging

350 g (12 oz) puff pastry, thawed if frozen

2 cloves of garlic, crushed

450 g (1 lb) leeks, washed, trimmed and cut into 2.5 cm (1 in) chunks

2 tbsp chopped fresh thyme

2 eggs, beaten

150 ml (¼ pt) single cream

salt and freshly ground black pepper

75 g (3 oz) grated red Leicester cheese

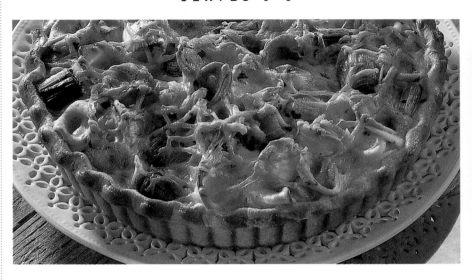

This dish is delicious both fresh out of the oven or served chilled on a hot summer's day with a crisp green salad.

Bring a large saucepan of water to the boil and add the orecchiette with a dash of olive oil; Cook for about 10 minutes, stirring occasionally, until tender. Drain and set aside.

Dredge the work surface with a little flour and roll out the pastry. Use to line a greased, 25 cm (10in) loose-bottomed fluted flan ring. Place in the refrigerator to chill for at least 10 minutes.

Preheat the oven to 190°C/375°F/Gas Mark 5. Heat the remaining olive oil in a large frying pan and sauté the garlic, leeks and thyme for about 5 minutes, stirring occasionally, until tender. Stir in the orecchiette and continue to cook for a further 2–3 minutes.

Place the beaten eggs in a mixing jug and whisk in the cream and salt and freshly ground black pepper.

Transfer the leek and pasta mixture to the pastry case, spreading out evenly. Pour over the egg and cream mixture, then sprinkle over with cheese. Bake for 30 minutes, until the mixture is firm and the pastry is crisp.

BABY CAULIFLOWER AND BROCCOLI CHEESE

SERVES 4

INGREDIENTS

350 g (12 oz) dried casareccia (long curled shapes)

dash of olive oil

50 g (2 oz) butter

salt and freshly ground black pepper

6 baby cauliflowers

6 baby broccoli spears

1 quantity Cheese Sauce (page 31)

45 ml (3 tbsp) dry white wine

30 ml (2 tbsp) double cream

75 g (3 oz) grated mature Cheddar cheese

Baby vegetables can be both formal and fun. To make this recipe suitable for children, omit the wine and cream from the sauce.

Bring a large saucepan of water to the boil and add the casareccia with a dash of olive oil. Cook for about 10 minutes, stirring occasionally, until tender. Drain and return to the saucepan with the butter and season with salt and freshly ground black pepper. Set aside, covered, to keep warm.

Bring a large saucepan of water to the boil and add the baby cauliflower and baby broccoli. Cook for about 5 minutes,

until tender. Drain and return to the saucepan, covered, to keep warm.

Place the Cheese Sauce in a saucepan and stir in the wine and cream. Heat gently, stirring constantly, for about 5 minutes.

To serve, divide the pasta between four warmed individual plates and arrange the baby vegetables on top. Pour over the Cheese Sauce and sprinkle with grated cheese. Serve immediately.

PROVENÇAL GREEN BEANS WITH PASTA

SERVES 4 – 6

A delicious way to serve green beans, piping hot with freshly grated Parmesan cheese.

Heat the oil in a large frying pan and sauté the garlic and onion for about 3 minutes, until softened. Add the thyme, beans, tomatoes, tomato purée, vegetable stock and wine, season with salt and freshly ground black pepper and stir well to combine. Cover and cook gently for 25–30 minutes, until the beans are tender. Remove the cover and cook for a further 5–8 minutes, stirring occasionally, until the sauce has thickened slightly.

Meanwhile, bring a large saucepan of water to the boil and add the pasta with a dash of olive oil. Cook for about 10 minutes, stirring occasionally, until tender. Drain and return to the saucepan. Toss in butter and freshly ground black pepper.

Serve the beans with the hot, buttered pasta and freshly grated Parmesan cheese.

INGREDIENTS

30 ml (2 tbsp) olive oil

3 cloves of garlic, crushed

1 onion, chopped

3 tbsp chopped fresh thyme

450 g (1 lb) haricot beans, topped and tailed

400-g (14-oz) can chopped tomatoes

50 g (2 oz) tomato purée

425 ml (¾ pt) vegetable stock

150 ml (¼ pt) dry red wine

salt and freshly ground black pepper

450 g (1 lb) dried pasta (any shapes)

25 g (1 oz) butter

freshly grated Parmesan cheese

PASTA PAELLA

SERVES 6 – 8

Bring a large saucepan of water to the boil and add the farfalle with the ground turmeric and a dash of olive oil. Cook for about 10 minutes, stirring occasionally, until tender. Drain, reserving the cooking liquid, and set aside.

Heat the remaining olive oil in a large frying pan and sauté the garlic and onion for about 3 minutes, until softened. Add the red pepper, carrots and sweetcorn and stir to combine. Cook for 2–3 minutes, then stir in the mangetout, asparagus tips, black olives and farfalle. Cook for 2–3 minutes, then sprinkle the flour over and mix into the vegetable mixture. Cook for 1 minute, then gradually stir in 425 ml (¾ pt) of the reserved pasta cooking liquid. Cook for 2–3 minutes, until the sauce is bubbling and thickened. Serve straight from the pan or transfer to a warmed serving dish.

INGREDIENTS

450 g (1 lb) dried farfalle (bows)

1 tsp ground turmeric

dash of olive oil, plus 45 ml (3 tbsp)

2 cloves of garlic, crushed

1 Spanish onion

1 red pepper, seeded and chopped

100 g (4 oz) baby carrots

100 g (4 oz) baby sweetcorn

100 g (4 oz) mangetout

100 g (4 oz) fresh asparagus tips

75 g (3 oz) black olives

15 g (½ oz) plain flour

SPINACH AND MUSHROOM LASAGNE

SERVES 6

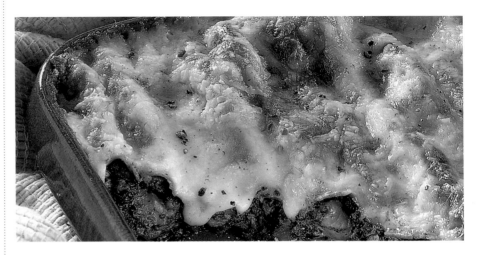

INGREDIENTS

butter, for greasing

225 g (8 oz) fresh lasagne

½ quantity Cheese Sauce (page 31)

50 g (2 oz) freshly grated Parmesan cheese

For the filling

30 ml (2 tbsp) olive oil

2 cloves of garlic, crushed

1 onion, chopped

225 g (8 oz) mushrooms, sliced

675 g (1½ lb) frozen spinach, thawed and well drained

good pinch of freshly grated nutmeg

450 g (1 lb) full-fat soft cheese

salt and freshly ground black pepper

Made in advance and put in the oven before the guests arrive, this is the perfect dish for entertaining. You can relax and enjoy the company while supper sees to itself.

Make the filling first. Heat the olive oil in a large frying pan and sauté the garlic and onion for about 3 minutes. Add the mushrooms and continue to cook for about 5 minutes, stirring occasionally. Add the spinach and nutmeg and cook for about 5 minutes, then stir in the soft cheese and season with salt and freshly ground black pepper. Cook for 3–4 minutes, until the cheese has melted and blended with the spinach mixture. Preheat the oven to 200°C/400°F/Gas Mark 6.

To assemble the lasagne, butter a lasagne dish and place a layer of lasagne on the bottom. Spoon some of the spinach mixture evenly over it, then add another layer of lasagne. Continue layering the pasta and spinach mixture alternately until both are used up, then pour the Cheese Sauce evenly over the top.

Sprinkle the Parmesan cheese over the lasagne and bake for about 40 minutes, until golden and bubbling.

VERDI VEGETABLES WITH VERMICELLI

SERVES 4 – 6

INGREDIENTS

350 g (12 oz) dried vermicelli (long, thin spaghetti)
dash of olive oil
25 g (1 oz) butter
350 g (12 oz) mangetout, sliced lengthways
225 g (8 oz) courgettes, shredded lengthways
75 g (3 oz) pimento-stuffed olives, sliced
salt and freshly ground black pepper
2 tbsp chopped fresh parsley
2 tbsp chopped fresh mint
squeeze of fresh lime juice

To garnish
fresh herbs
lime slices

A lovely summer recipe to be eaten warm or cold, with chunks of crusty French bread.

Bring a large saucepan of water to the boil and add the vermicelli with a dash of olive oil. Cook for about 5 minutes, stirring occasionally, until tender. Drain and set aside.

Melt the butter in a large frying pan and sauté the sliced mangetout and the courgettes for about 5 minutes, stirring occasionally.

Add the remaining ingredients except the lime juice to the vegetable mixture and cook for a further 5 minutes, stirring occasionally. Mix in the vermicelli and cook for 2–3 minutes, until heated through. Squeeze the fresh lime juice over the mixture and serve, garnished with fresh herbs and lime slices.

STUFFED COURGETTES

SERVES 4–6

A delicious combination of tender courgette and fresh coriander mixed with a sweet soy sauce. You can make the filling and the sauce a day in advance. Reheat the sauce while the courgettes are baking.

Bring a large saucepan of water to the boil and add the vermicelli with a dash of olive oil. Cook for about 5 minutes, stirring occasionally, until tender. Drain and set aside.

Cut a thin slice lengthways along the top of each courgette and chop this piece finely. Using a teaspoon, scoop out the flesh from the middle of the courgette and chop roughly. Arrange the hollowed courgettes in a shallow ovenproof dish and set aside. Preheat the oven to 200°C/400°F/Gas Mark 6.

To make the filling, place the sweet soy sauce and the garlic in a large frying pan and heat gently. Cook for about 1 minute, then stir in the mushrooms. Cook for about 5 minutes, stirring occasionally, then add the coriander. Cook for a further 2–3 minutes, then stir in the chopped walnuts and season to taste with salt and freshly ground black pepper. Simmer for 1–2 minutes, then stir in the cooked vermicelli.

Remove from the heat and, using a teaspoon, stuff the courgettes with the filling, placing any extra around the courgettes in the dish. Cover the dish with aluminium foil and bake for 25–30 minutes, until the courgettes are tender.

Meanwhile, to make the sauce, place all the ingredients in a food processor or blender and purée until smooth. Transfer to a small saucepan and heat gently until warm. Remove the stuffed courgettes from the oven and serve with the coriander sauce, garnished with finely chopped walnuts.

INGREDIENTS

4 oz dried vermicelli (very thin spaghetti), broken into small pieces
dash of olive oil
4 medium-sized courgettes
finely chopped walnuts, to garnish

For the Filling

¼ pt sweet soy sauce
1 clove of garlic, minced
2 oz mushrooms, very finely chopped
3 tbsp fresh chopped coriander
1 oz shelled walnuts, very finely chopped
salt and freshly ground black pepper

For the Sauce

4 tbsp olive oil
2 cloves of garlic, crushed
1 oz chopped fresh coriander
salt and freshly ground black pepper
3 tbsp vegetable stock

GNOCCHETTI SARDI WITH BROCCOLI AND TOMATOES

SERVES 4

INGREDIENTS

350 g (12 oz) dried gnocchetti sardi (small dumpling shapes)
dash of olive oil
75 g (3 oz) unsalted butter
350 g (12 oz) small broccoli florets
1 clove of garlic, chopped
2 tsp chopped fresh rosemary
2 tsp chopped fresh oregano
salt and freshly ground black pepper
200 g (7 oz) can chopped tomatoes
15 ml (1 tbsp) tomato purée
fresh herbs, to garnish

A lovely light lunch or supper dish. Choose vivid green, tightly packed heads of broccoli and cook as briefly as possible to retain the color and crisp texture.

Bring a large saucepan of water to the boil and add the gnocchetti sardi with a dash of olive oil. Cook for about 6 minutes, stirring occasionally until tender. Drain and return to the saucepan, covered, to keep warm.

Meanwhile, melt the butter in a large frying pan. Add the broccoli, garlic, rosemary and oregano and season with salt and freshly ground black pepper. Cover and cook gently for about 5 minutes, until tender.

Add the chopped tomatoes and tomato purée and stir. Add the gnocchetti sardi, mix together lightly, then serve immediately, garnished with fresh herbs.

TOMATO AND PASTA SALAD

SERVES 6 – 8

INGREDIENTS

550 g (1¼ lb) fresh orecchiette (ears)

dash of olive oil

450 g (1 lb) red and yellow tomatoes, chopped

15 cm (6 inch) piece cucumber, chopped

175 g (6 oz) feta cheese, chopped

5 tbsp chopped fresh coriander

2 tbsp chopped fresh basil

For the Dressing

15 ml (1 tbsp) white wine vinegar

60 ml (4 tbsp) olive oil

2 cloves of garlic, crushed

salt and freshly ground black pepper

To Garnish

cherry tomatoes

fresh coriander sprigs

Oriecchiette are small ear-shaped pasta. If they are not available, gnocchi pasta shapes (dumplings) will work just as well.

Bring a large saucepan of water to the boil and add the orecchiette with a dash of olive oil. Cook for about 5 minutes, stirring occasionally, until tender. Drain and rinse under cold running water. Drain again and set aside.

Place the orecchiette in a large mixing bowl and add the remaining salad ingredients. Mix to combine. To make the dressing, place all the ingredients in a screw-top jar and shake well. Pour the dressing over the salad and toss to coat. Serve garnished with cherry tomatoes and coriander sprigs.

ASPARAGUS RAVIOLI WITH TOMATO SAUCE

SERVES 6

A dinner-party dish which can be made in advance – the ravioli can even be put in the freezer several weeks before the party and cooked from frozen. The sauce can be made several hours ahead and reheated before serving.

Keep the fresh pasta dough covered with clingfilm at room temperature and the Tomato Sauce in a saucepan, ready to reheat before serving.

To make the filling, heat the olive oil in a frying pan and sauté the garlic and onion for about 3 minutes, until the onion has softened. Add the chopped fresh asparagus and season with salt and freshly ground black pepper. Sauté the asparagus mixture for about 10 minutes, until softened. Set aside and allow to cool completely.

To make the ravioli, cut the pasta dough in half. Roll out one half to a rectangle slightly larger than 35 x 25 cm (14 x 10 inches). Trim the edges of the dough neatly. Cover the rectangle with the clingfilm to prevent it drying out. Roll out the other half of the dough to the same measurements. Do not trim the edges.

Place half teaspoonfuls of the filling mixture in lines, spaced about 2 cm (¾ inch) apart, all over the trimmed rectangle of pasta dough. Brush the beaten egg lightly, in lines around the filling mixture, to make the square shapes for the ravioli.

Lay the other rectangle of pasta dough on top and, starting at one end, seal in the filling by lightly pressing the dough, pushing out any trapped air and gently flattening the filling, making little packets. Using a sharp knife or pastry wheel, cut down and then across in lines around the filling to make the square ravioli shapes.

To cook the ravioli, bring a large saucepan of water to the boil and add the ravioli with a dash of olive oil. Cook for about 6 minutes, stirring occasionally, until tender. Drain and set aside.

Meanwhile, reheat the Tomato Sauce. Serve the ravioli with the Tomato Sauce, sprinkled with chopped fresh herbs.

INGREDIENTS

½ quantity Pasta Dough with 1 tbsp tomato paste
beaten into the eggs
1 quantity Tomato Sauce
1 egg, beaten, for brushing
dash of olive oil
chopped fresh herbs, to garnish

For the Filling

2 tbsp olive oil
1 clove of garlic, crushed
1 onion, very finely chopped
299g (8oz) fresh asparagus, very finely chopped
salt and freshly ground black pepper

Cheese Sauce 600ml (1pt)

25g (1 oz) butter or margarine
25g (1 oz) flour
600ml (1pt) warm milk
1 tsp Dijon mustard
100g (4 oz) grated mature Chedder Cheese
salt and freshly ground black pepper

Tomato sauce

As above but omit mustard and cheese and stir in 3 tbsp tomato paste

Pasta Dough 625g (1¼lb)

300g (12 oz) flour
1 tbsp salt
4 tbsp sunflower oil
1 tbsp water
3 eggs

Chapter Three

Side Dishes

Glazed Carrots with Coriander

■

Aubergine Dip with Sunflower Seeds

■

Pineapple and Chilli Pepper Rice

■

Paprika Potatoes in Spicy Sauce

■

Mushroom, Pear, Green Bean
and Walnut Salad

■

Sweet and Sour Red Cabbage

■

Moroccan Carrot salad

■

Haricot Beans with Tomato sauce
and Onion

■

Hot Beet in Yogurt and Mustard Sauce

■

Japanese Style Vegetable Tempura

GLAZED CARROTS WITH CORIANDER

SERVES 4

INGREDIENTS

625g (1¼ lb) carrots, scraped and cut into
julienne strips
4 celery stalks, thinly sliced
juice and grated rind of ½ orange
120ml (4 fl oz) vegetable stock
1 tsp coriander seeds, lightly crushed
salt and finely ground black pepper

Garnish

1 tbsp chopped coriander or mint

There's a special affinity between carrots and oranges – and it's not just because of their colour. This is a minus-the-fat version of glazed carrots, pepped up with ground coriander seeds.

Put the carrots, celery, orange juice and rind, stock, and coriander seeds into a pan, and season with salt and pepper. Bring to the boil and simmer uncovered over a low heat for 15 minutes or until the vegetables are tender and most of the liquid has been absorbed. Take care that the pan does not dry out. If it does, add a little more orange juice or stock.

Sprinkle with the chopped herb and serve hot.

AUBERGINE DIP WITH SUNFLOWER SEEDS
SERVES 4

INGREDIENTS

1 tbsp sunflower seeds

59g (2oz) grated aubergine

2–3 garlic cloves, crushed

pinch of salt

3–4 tbsp skimmed milk

50g (2oz) low-fat plain yogurt

1 tsp artificial sweetener

¼ tsp cumin seeds, crushed

¼ tsp freshly ground black pepper

25g (1oz) chopped tomato

few mint leaves or pinch of dried mint

pinch of chilli powder

Put the sunflower seeds into a heavy-bottomed frying pan and heat them over a medium heat. Move the seeds around continuously with a wooden spoon, roasting them for 1 minute. Switch the heat off, but keep on stirring the seeds as the pan cools, then leave them to cool completely.

Pour ¼ cup of water into a small saucepan, together with the aubergine, garlic, and a pinch of salt, then bring it to a boil. Cook for 2 to 3 minutes, until the aubergine is softened to a pulp, then remove the pan from the heat and leave it to one side to cool.

Beat the milk and yogurt together in a bowl until smooth, then add the aubergine, sugar, cumin seeds, and pepper and blend well.

Add the tomato and mint leaves or dried mint.

Sprinkle the chilli powder over the top and garnish with the sunflower seeds just before serving.

PINEAPPLE AND CHILLI PEPPER RICE

SERVES 4

Cut the pineapple in half lengthways through the plume and scoop out the flesh. Reserve the two halves. Discard the central core, dice the remaining flesh and reserve.

Heat the oil in a pan and sauté the red bell pepper and courgettes for 5 minutes, or until softened. Add the spring onionsand sauté for a further minute. Stir the rice with the chilli peppers, seasoning, and the reserved pineapple flesh.

Heat gently, stirring occasionally, for 5 minutes, or until hot. Then stir in the pine nuts and coriander. Pile into the reserved pineapple shells and serve with grated low-fat cheese.

INGREDIENTS

1 large or 2 medium fresh pineapples
2 tbsp sunflower oil
1 red bell pepper, seeded, and chopped
200g (8 oz) courgettes, trimmed and diced
6 spring onions, trimmed and sliced diagonally
250g (10 oz) cooked long-grain rice
6 jarred jalapeño chilli peppers, drained and chopped
salt and freshly ground black pepper
2 tbsp pine nuts, toasted
3 tbsp freshly chopped coriander
grated low-fat cheese, to serve

PAPRIKA POTATOES IN SPICY SAUCE

SERVES 6

INGREDIENTS

1⅛ kg (2¼ lb) potatoes, scrubbed

salt

1 tsp sunflower oil

1 medium onion, chopped

1 clove garlic, crushed

1 tbsp paprika

300ml (½ pt) vegetable stock

200g (8-oz) can tomatoes, chopped

½ tsp caraway seeds

1 small green bell pepper, cored, seeded, and chopped

freshly ground black pepper

3 tbsp plain low-fat yogurt

Garnish

2 tbsp chopped parsley

The potatoes can be pre-cooked and left in the spicy sauce, ready to be reheated while the main dish is cooking.

Cook the potatoes in boiling salted water for 5 minutes, then drain them. Unless they are very small, cut the potatoes into medium-sized slices.

Heat the oil in a saucepan, and fry the onion and garlic over medium heat for about 3 minutes, until the onion is soft. Stir in the paprika, and cook for 1 minute. Pour on the stock, and add the tomatoes (including juice), caraway seeds, and green bell pepper. Season with salt and pepper, add the potatoes, and stir well. Bring to a boil and simmer, uncovered, for 20 minutes, until the potatoes are tender and the sauce has thickened.

Stir in the yogurt, taste the sauce, and adjust the seasoning if necessary. Serve hot, sprinkled with the parsley.

MUSHROOM, PEAR, GREEN BEAN, AND WALNUT SALAD

SERVES 6

INGREDIENTS

125g (¼ lb) green beans, trimmed and halved

2 ripe pears, peeled, cored, and sliced

2 tsp lemon juice

250g (½ lb) button mushrooms, trimmed, halved, or sliced

1 small lettuce, washed, and drained and torn into small pieces

25g (1oz) walnut halves

Dressing

1 tbsp sunflower oil

3 tbsp plain low-fat yogurt

1 tbsp clear honey

salt and freshly ground black pepper

This mixed fruit, vegetable, and nut salad, with its sweet-and-sour dressing, makes a substantial accompaniment to a plain dish but can also be served alone as a first course.

Cook the green beans in boiling water for 2 minutes, then drain them in a colander. Run cold water through them to prevent further cooking, then drain again.

Sprinkle the pear slices with the lemon juice, then toss them in a bowl with the beans, mushrooms, lettuce, and walnuts.

Mix the dressing ingredients, pour over the salad, and toss thoroughly. Serve.

INGREDIENTS

2 tbsp vegetable oil

1 onion, cut in half and thinly sliced

2 dessert apples, peeled, cored, and thinly sliced

1 red cabbage, about 750g (1½ lb), quartered, cored, and shredded

60ml (4 tbsp) red-wine vinegar

2 to 3 tbsp light brown sugar

120ml (4floz) vegetable stock or water

salt and freshly ground black pepper

SWEET AND SOUR RED CABBAGE

SERVES 6

Cabbage is an important ingredient in many kitchens, especially in Russia and Central Europe. This braised sweet-and-sour cabbage dish is also delicious served cold. If you want to make the green cabbage version, use white-wine vinegar or lemon juice and white sugar.

In a large, heavy-bottomed, non-aluminium pan, over medium-high heat, heat oil. Add onion and cook until soft and golden, 5–7 minutes. Add sliced apples and cook until beginning to brown, 2–3 minutes.

Add cabbage and remaining ingredients. Simmer, covered, stirring occasionally and adding water if necessary until cabbage is tender, 30–40 minutes. Uncover and cook until liquid is absorbed. Spoon into a serving bowl.

MOROCCAN CARROT SALAD

SERVES 4

This is a favourite Middle Eastern salad, popular in Israel. It is sweet and spicy, as well as being colourful. Raw grated carrots can be used, but traditionally the carrots are cooked first.

In a food processor fitted with a grater blade, or with a hand-grater, grate carrots into a large bowl. Set aside.

In a medium frying pan, over medium-low heat, heat oil. Add chopped garlic and cook until garlic begins to soften and colour, 2–3 minutes. Add salt, cumin, red chilli pepper flakes, cayenne or red pepper sauce, and sugar, stirring to blend.

Stir in chopped parsley and lemon juice. Slowly pour in ½–¾ cup of the carrot cooking liquid. Bring to the boil and simmer 3–5 minutes. Pour over carrots. Cool to room temperature.

Cover and refrigerate 6–8 hours or overnight. Spoon into a serving bowl and garnish with parsley sprigs.

INGREDIENTS

500g (1 lb carrots), peeled and cooked until just tender, cooking liquid reserved
2 tbsp vegetable oil
2 garlic cloves, peeled and finely chopped
1 tsp salt
1½ tsp cumin
½ tsp red chili pepper flakes, cayenne pepper, or red pepper sauce
1 tsp sugar
2 to 3 tbsp chopped fresh parsley
3 to 4 tbsp lemon juice

Garnish

fresh parsley sprigs

HARICOT BEANS WITH TOMATO SAUCE AND ONION

SERVES 4

INGREDIENTS

200g (8 oz) haricot beans, soaked overnight, and drained

3 tbsp virgin olive oil

3 garlic cloves, finely chopped

3 tbsp chopped parsley

1 tbsp chopped mixed thyme and rosemary

1 bay leaf

pinch of dried oregano

¼–½ tsp crushed red chilli pepper flakes

1 cup water

2 large tomatoes, peeled, seeded, and diced

salt and freshly ground black pepper

¼ Spanish onion, very finely chopped

finely chopped coriander or parsley, to serve

This recipe is distinguished from other beans in tomato sauce recipes by the addition of a mound of finely chopped raw onion and some chopped coriander or parsley to each portion as it is served. This really livens up the dish, but it is important to use a mild onion.

Put the beans into a saucepan and just cover with water. Boil for 10 minutes and then simmer for about 50 minutes or until the beans are tender.

Heat the oil, garlic, herbs, and crushed red pepper gently for 4 minutes. Add the water, bring to the boil, then cover and simmer for 5 minutes. Stir in the tomatoes, cover again and simmer for 4 minutes.

Drain the beans and stir into the tomato mixture gently. Season and simmer for 4–5 minutes.

Ladle the beans and sauce into four warmed soup plates and put a small mound of onion and some coriander or parsley in the centre of each.

HOT BEET IN YOGURT AND MUSTARD SAUCE

SERVES 4

INGREDIENTS

500g (1 lb) small beets, trimmed and
scrubbed
salt
120ml (4floz) low-fat yogurt
1 tsp cornflour
2 tsp wholegrain mustard
1 clove garlic, crushed
1 tbsp chopped mint
freshly ground black pepper

Garnish

2 spring onions, trimmed and thinly sliced

A popular salad vegetable in many countries, beets have an equally attractive role to play as a hot vegetable accompaniment. This dish has middle-Eastern origins.

Cook the beets in boiling salted water for 30 minutes, or until they are tender. Drain them and, as soon as they are cool enough to handle, scrape them. If the vegetables are very small, they are best left whole; others may be sliced or diced.

Mix the yogurt with the cornflour, and put in a pan with the mustard and garlic. Heat gently, then stir In the beets. When they have heated through, stir in the mint and season with pepper. Serve warm in a heated dish, garnished with the spring onion slices.

45

JAPANESE-STYLE VEGETABLE TEMPURA

SERVES 6

Maximize the colour and texture of a variety of vegetables in this crisp Japanese dish. It can be served to complement baked or broiled dishes, or presented as the main dish with brown rice.

First make the sauce. Place the ginger, soy sauce, and honey in a flameproof serving bowl, pour on the boiling water, and stir well. Leave to cool.

To make the batter, mix the dry ingredients in a bowl and gradually pour on the water, beating all the time.

Toss all the vegetables in the flour to coat them; shake off any excess. Heat the oil in a wok or deep-frying pan.

Using a slotted spoon, dip the vegetables in the batter a few at a time, and allow the excess to drain back into the bowl. Fry the vegetables in several batches, reheating the oil between each one, until they are evenly golden brown.

Lift out the vegetables and toss them on kitchen towels to drain off excess oil. Serve at once with the sauce in a separate dish.

INGREDIENTS

Sauce

5cm (2 in) piece fresh root ginger, peeled and grated

2 tbsp soy sauce

1 tsp clear honey

120ml (4floz) boiling water

Vegetables

1½ cup cauliflower florets

2 large carrots, scraped and cut into julienne strips

1 large onion, sliced into rings

1 red bell pepper, cored, seeded, and sliced

125g (¼lb) small button mushrooms, trimmed and halved

flour, for coating

sunflower oil, for deep frying

Batter

50g (2oz) whole-wheat flour

2 tbsp fine cornmeal

2 tbsp arrowroot

300ml (10floz) water

CHAPTER FOUR

DESSERTS

INGREDIENTS

500g (1 lb) rhubarb, trimmed and cut into
2.5cm (1-inch) lengths
grated rind and juice of 1 orange
1 tbsp water
12g (½oz) pitted dates, chopped
2 tbsp clear honey

Topping

75g (3oz) whole-wheat breadcrumbs
50g (2oz) rolled oats
4 tbsp polyunsaturated margarine, melted
4 tbsp light brown unrefined sugar

BAKED RHUBARB WITH OAT TOPPING
SERVES 4

Family members who like old-fashioned puddings will love this sticky-toffee fruit layer topped with a healthful and delicious crunchy mixture.

Set the oven to 350°F/180°C/Gas mark 4
Place the rhubarb, orange juice and rind, water, dates, and honey in a 1½ l (2½ pint) ovenproof dish.

For the topping, mix together the breadcrumbs, oats, margarine, and sugar, and spread the topping over the fruit. Bake in the oven for about 35 minutes, until the topping is golden. Serve piping hot.

INGREDIENTS

25g (1oz) light brown unrefined sugar

1 small orange

600ml (1 pt) water

500g (1 lb) cooking apples, peeled, cored, and sliced

125g (¼ lb) dried apricot pieces, soaked overnight and drained

2 tbsp powdered gelatin

Decoration

herb leaves

APRICOT RING MOULD

SERVES 6

With its golden colour and glistening texture, this is a very appealing dessert, and one that has the hidden benefit of a high fibre content provided by the apricots.

Put the sugar, a strip of the orange rind, and the water in a pan and bring it slowly to the boil, stirring occasionally to dissolve the sugar. Fast-boil for 3 minutes, and then add the apple slices and poach them over low heat for about 8 minutes, or until they become translucent and are just tender. Lift out the apple slices with a slotted spoon and set them aside.

Add the apricots and the juice of the orange to the syrup, bring to the boil, and simmer for 20 minutes or until the fruit is tender. Discard the orange rind, and purée the fruit thoroughly in a blender or food processor.

Sprinkle the gelatin on to 3 tablespoons of hot water in a small bowl. Stand the bowl in a pan of hot water, and stir to dissolve the crystals. Stir the solution into the apricot purée and set aside to cool.

Rinse a 1.2l (2-pint) ring mould with cold water. Arrange the apple slices in the base, and spoon on the apricot purée. Cover the mould and chill it in the refrigerator for about 2 hours, or until it has set firmly.

Run a knife around the sides of the mould, and dip it quickly in and out of hot water. Place a flat serving plate over the mold, invert it quickly, and shake to release the fruit. Decorate the mould with herb leaves.

MELON AND WALNUT COMPOTE

SERVES 6

Versions of this simple dessert are eaten from Greece through Georgia and Armenia to Uzbekistan.

Place the melon cubes, with any juice, in a bowl. Add the honey and toss to coat lightly. Stir in the walnuts. Divide the mixture among individual bowls.

INGREDIENTS

---

2 small cantaloupe or honeydew melons, halved, seeded, and cubed

360ml (1⅛pt) honey

150g (6oz) walnuts, chopped

BLACKCURRANT SORBET

SERVES 4

INGREDIENTS

500g (1 lb) blackcurrants, fresh or frozen

4 tbsp clear honey

25g (1oz) sugar

120ml (4floz) water

2 egg whites

Decoration

mint sprigs (optional)

Put the blackcurrants, honey, sugar, and water into a saucepan, and bring slowly to the boil, stirring occasionally. Simmer for 15 minutes, or until the fruit is soft. Allow to cool.

Rub the fruit and juice through a sieve, and place it in a metal ice-cube tray or plastic freezer box. Cover with foil or a lid, and freeze for 1–2 hours, until the mixture is mushy and starting to set on the outside.

Beat the egg whites until stiff. Turn the fruit purée out into a chilled bowl and fold in the egg whites.

Return the mixture to the container, cover, and freeze for another 2 hours, or until firm. Stir it once or twice.

To serve, allow the sorbet to soften a little in the refrigerator for about 30 minutes. Spoon or scoop it into four individual serving glasses, and top each one with a mint sprig if you wish.

ORANGE SORBET

SERVES 6

INGREDIENTS

50g (2oz) sugar
grated zest and juice of 1 lemon
grated zest of 3 oranges
½ l (1pt) fresh-squeezed orange juice, strained
2 egg whites, beaten to soft peaks
fresh mint leaves for garnish
Cointreau for serving

In a small heavy saucepan, combine sugar, lemon and orange zests and 1 cup water. Slowly bring to the boil, stirring until sugar dissolves. Cook 5 minutes; remove from heat and cool and refrigerate 3–4 hours or overnight.

Combine lemon and orange juices with the chilled syrup and, if you like, strain for a very smooth sorbet.

If using an ice-cream machine, freeze according to manufacturer's directions.

Alternatively, put into a metal bowl and freeze 3–4 hours until semifrozen. Into a food processor fitted with metal blade. Scrape the semifrozen mixture; process until light and creamy, 30–45 seconds. Return to the metal bowl and freeze another 1½ hours. Scrape into food processor again and process with beaten egg whites until well mixed and light and creamy - 30 seconds. Freeze 3–4 hours until completely firm.

Soften 5 minutes at room temperature before scooping into individual serving glasses. Garnish with a few mint leaves and pass the liqueur, allowing each guest to pour a little over sorbet.

YOGURT DELIGHT

SERVES 4

Mix the yogurt, orange zest, and 2–3 tbsp of the honey, then divide it between four dishes and chill well.

Melt the butter, then stir fry the pistachios and Brazils with the raisins for 3 minutes. Add the pears and continue to stir fry for about 3 minutes, or until the pears are lightly cooked. Stir in the apricots and orange juice and bring to the boil. Boil, stirring, for 2 minutes to reduce the orange juice.

Stir in the grapes and remaining honey (or to taste) and heat through briefly. Spoon the fruit and nut mixture on top of the chilled yogurt and serve at once.

INGREDIENTS

150g (6oz) cups low-fat yogurt
grated zest and juice of 1 orange
60-120ml (2-4floz) clear honey
knob of unsalted butter
25g (1oz) shelled pistachio nuts
25g (1oz) Brazil nuts, roughly chopped
25g (1oz) raisins
2 firm pears, peeled, cored and diced
40g (1½oz) ready-to-eat dried apricots, sliced
25g (1oz) seedless grapes, halved

INGREDIENTS

1 ogen or canteloupe melon, seeded and
sliced in thin wedges and peeled
3 sweet seedless oranges, peeled and
segmented, juice reserved
1 mango, peeled and thinly sliced
24 fresh lychees, peeled, or 1 400g (16-oz)
can lychees in their own juice
12 Medjool dates, cut in half lengthwise and
pitted
1 pomegranate, cut in half, seeds reserved
(optional)

Garnish

fresh mint leaves

SLICED EXOTIC FRUITS WITH DATES
SERVES 6

Fruit salad has always been a popular dessert and almost any seasonal fruits are delicious sliced or cut up together in their natural juices or with a fruit purée. This is not a traditional fruit salad, but a selection of exotic fruits, sliced and served together. Ogen melons from Israel are as sweet as sugar, as are the Israeli oranges. California produces a wonderful variety of date, the Medjool date, which is recommended for this dish.

Arrange slices of melon on each of six individual plates in a fan shape. Arrange peeled orange segments and mango slices in an attractive pattern over the melon slices.

Evenly distribute fresh or canned lychees over fruit and sprinkle on some reserved fruits from all fruits.

Arrange four date halves on each plate and sprinkle with the pomegranate seeds, if using. Garnish with fresh mint leaves and serve.

BLACKBERRY AND WHISKY OATIE

SERVES 4

INGREDIENTS

30g (1½oz) rolled oat

5 tbsp Scotch whisky

3 tbsp clear honey

25g (1 oz) low-fat cottage cheese, sieved

30ml (1 floz) plain low-fat yogurt

1 tsp grated orange rind

250g (½ lb) blackberries, hulled

Decoration

fresh mint

This dessert has its origins in Scotland, where the combination of oats and whisky strikes a chord of national pride.

Put the oats and whisky into a bowl, cover, and set aside for at least 2 hours, or overnight if it is more convenient.

Beat together the honey, cheese, and yogurt and stir in the orange rind. Stir in most of the blackberries.

In four tall glass dessert dishes, make layers of the fruit mixture and oats, beginning and ending with the fruit. Decorate each glass with a few reserved berries and a sprig of fresh mint. Serve chilled.